PART I

INTRODUCTION

The majority of people will view Presidents of the United States as if they are higher than them, like they are on a pedestal. Although they may not be as popular today as Lincoln's, we have many media outlets to show their weaknesses and sins at a moment's notice. We are also ready to burn them to the ground for the same sins and weaknesses that many of us are committed. This author believes that every sitting president or congressman was created equal.

Abraham Lincoln was the same person when he met his fellow servants. He didn't feel superior to anyone.

This book will tell you about his humble beginnings, his family, his struggles with moving as a child, his desire to go to school, and his eventual marriage to Mary Todd.

~

We will learn about their four children and the future for each one.

~

Find out how Mary Todd Lincoln's insaneness affected her, her children and President Lincoln.

~

This is how he rose to the top of politics and became President. You will learn that he was loved by some and hated by others.

~

Here are some gossips and rumors about Mary Lincoln and Abraham Lincoln. You can decide what you believe.

~

Enjoy the contents of this book.

PART II

————

ABRAHAM LINCOLN'S EARLY DAYS

<<I am a slow walker, but I never walk back.>>

Abraham Lincoln

Abraham Lincoln was born in this world on February 12, 1809 in Kentucky, Hardin County. The Lincoln's moved to Knob Creek Farm in 1811. Knob Creek Farm is now part of the Lincoln Birthplace Historic Site. The family moved to southern Indiana seven years later in 1816. Thomas Lincoln and Nancy Hanks, his parents, had two more children.

Although Nancy Hanks' family tree is difficult to trace, it appears that Nancy was likely illegitimate. She was described as thin-breasted, sad, stoopshouldered and religious.

After Nancy's death, Tom Lincoln was overwhelmed by caring for, farming, and hunting food to feed his children.

If Abraham Lincoln were alive today, he would say that his boyhood was his most difficult time after the death of his biological mother in the fall 1818. Abe was nine years of age when his mother died. He had to face cold winters without the warmth of his mother's love.

Abe and his sister were often left alone, filthy, skinny, and beaten by their father. They were abandoned by Tom Lincoln for six months. But he returned with a wife.

Sarah Bush Johnston Lincoln was the widow who brought two boys and two girls with her. She was full of energy and had lots to give. Because she treated Tom's and her children as if they were her own, she managed the house with an impartial hand. Sarah loved Abraham and she was fond of him. Later on, he would refer to her as his "angel mom".

Thomas, Lincoln's father, was a weaver's apprentice who had immigrated from England to Massachusetts in 1637. Thomas was not as wealthy as some of Lincoln's but he was still a strong pioneer with a hard-core attitude.

Abraham's younger brother Thomas died in infancy. Lincoln was the older brother of Sarah, his sister.

Abraham and his parents moved to Indiana in 1817 after a land dispute. Because of all the confusion about all the land grants, and purchase agreements, which were freely handed out, the issue of the land conflict was magnified. This led to numerous legal disputes over land ownership in Kentucky.

The Lincoln's moved from Illinois to Perry County in 1817. They "squatted" land on public land. Their homestead site was considered "fairly wild" and difficult to farm. This was what drove Tom Lincoln to hunt for food for his family. Thomas Lincoln constructed a log cabin with just one room. It had no floor or furniture. All of the family slept on corn husks as their bedding.

Abraham's childhood memories are his earliest. Abraham's father, Thomas, had helped him plant corn and pumpkin seeds. One of his most memorable memories was about a flash flood.

Thomas Lincoln was able to save enough money through hard work and perseverance to purchase the plot of land he wanted.

Even though it was brief, there was a time when a small school was close to their home. Abraham Lincoln was reported to have walked nine miles each way to get to school. It was taking him between two and three hours each direction.

Abraham Lincoln learned the law by himself, and passed the Law Bar Exam in 1836.

PART III

THE LINCOLNS MOVE TO ILLINOIS

<<The philosophy of the school room in one generation will be the philosophy of government in the next.>>

Abraham Lincoln

March 1830 saw the Lincoln family move again. This time, it was to Illinois. Lincoln drove the oxen team.

Abe was 21 years old, and was about start his life on his merit. Six foot four, he was strong and muscular at six feet four. Abe was well-known for his strength and ability to use an ax. A man like Abe is the ideal choice for frontier women?

Abraham had a charming, slow backwoods twang. He walked cautiously, with a flat-footed and long-stride like a plowman. Abraham was a good-natured, but also moody. He was also very skilled at mimicking stories and was a magnet for friends. He had not yet demonstrated his other exceptional abilities.

Lincoln arrived in Illinois with no desire to be a farmer. He tried several occupations. Lincoln tried his hand at being a railroad splitter and a flatboat man, as well as helping to clear fences for his father.

He was a flatboatman and made his way to New Orleans, Louisiana. He returned to Illinois and settled in New Salem, an area of twenty-five families located along the Sangamon River.

He worked in New Salem as a surveyor and postmaster. Abe knew that the Black Hawk War (1832), was near, so he enlisted as a volunteer. He was elected captain of his company immediately.

Abraham joked that he never saw any "fighting, living Indians" during the war, but that his bloodiest fights were with mosquitoes.

He wanted to be a politician and a legislator, but he was defeated in his first attempt. However, he kept trying again and was re-elected to the state assembly. He considered becoming a blacksmith, but he decided to become a lawyer. He was already proficient in grammar and mathematics, and he was now beginning to read the law books. He passed the bar exam and began to practice law in 1836.

He made the move to Springfield, Illinois in the following year because there were more opportunities for him to practice law than New Salem. He formed a partnership initially with John T. Stuart. Later, he became partners with Stephan T. Logan. He worked alongside William H. Herndon in 1844. Lincoln was nearly ten years older than Herndon. He was also more educated, more emotionally involved at the bar, and seemed more extreme in his views.

Lincoln's partnership was with Herndon, but it was not a smooth one. They never kept any records about their business. They split the money between them when either one of them was paid. There are no records of money quarrels. This would be unacceptable in today's business world at so many levels.

Lincoln was earning $1200 to $1500 per year after he moved to Springfield. The state governor received only $1200 per year, while the circuit judges earned $750. Lincoln needed to be busy. He realized that he had to not only work in Springfield, but also keep up with the circuit judge. Abraham traveled hundreds of miles by buggy and horseback every fall and spring, crossing sparsely populated prairies to get from one county to the other. Most cases seemed to be petty, and there were very few fees.

Lincoln's practice started making more money after the railroads were built in 1850. Lincoln began lobbying to bring in the Illinois Central Railroad. He also helped obtain a charter from the state. Lincoln was retained by the railroad as their regular attorney.

Lincoln received $5,000 after defending the Railroad against McLean County's taxation of railroad property. He had to sue McLean county to collect. He began to handle cases for banks and other railroads, manufacturing, mercantile, and insurance companies.

He saved the bridge over the Mississippi River from being destroyed by the interests who wanted to remove it. It was one of his most memorable achievements. Lincoln's business grew to include patent litigation and criminal trials. A murder trial was one of Lincoln's most famous lawsuits.

One witness claimed that he saw Duff Armstrong, a man Lincoln believed to have played a role in the murder. Lincoln used an almanac from a farmer to show that it was too dark for the witness to see any explicit information. Lincoln was acquitted after making a sincere appeal to the jury that was so touching.

It was around twenty years after Lincoln became a lawyer, and was noted as one of the most successful lawyers in Illinois.

Lincoln had a special way about him that enabled him to see beyond the lawsuit's heart and to see the truth and fairness of the case. He was also noted for his practical common sense, but his deep understanding.

Abraham Lincoln met Ann Rutledge while he was in New Salem. He seemed to be fond of her and he mourned the loss of Ann Rutledge, who was 22 years old at her death in 1835. Many stories have been written about their great romance after she died.

Some people feel there is no historical support for this belief. Abraham Lincoln began to flirt with Mary Owens half-heartedly about a year after Rutledge died. She said that Abe was lacking in certain areas that would allow a woman to be happy. She then rejected his proposal for marriage.

Robert Rutledge began a letter by telling Ann about John McNamar's engagement. Then, Ann had a very colorful drama about her alleged relationship to Abe Lincoln.

McNamar was a New Salem merchant who was wealthy. He had also been courting Ann and had allegedly secured an engagement. To take care of family matters, he returned to the east. He seemed to be writing letters to Ann for a while, but then suddenly the letters stopped coming. He seemed to have left Ann hanging, and was publicly embarrassed. Lincoln appears to be at her rescue.

Robert continues to tell us that Abe Lincoln visited Ann and kept her interested, which led to him asking her to marry her. It was an honorable, conditional release to end McNamar's contract.

According to legend, David Rutledge wanted Ann for the marriage to be finalized, but she was hesitant to do so until McNamar could see her face-to-face. McNamar didn't return to Ann's house until after she had died, while Abe was living there in New Salem.

Abe Lincoln seemed to have suffered a terrible mental effect. He became depressed and many of his closest friends worried that he would lose his mind. It seemed that Abe had a very tender relationship with Ann Rutledge (the dead) because of his depression.

There were Rutledge family members who were firm about Lincoln's engagement to their sister.

Lincoln was there for Ann Rutledge when she was so ill and died, and also during her funeral. Ann Rutledge had already agreed to marry Lincoln before she fell ill. However, she wanted to wait at least one year before they were married to be eligible to join the Bar. Ann Rutledge passed away before the year was over.

Lincoln was so affected after Anne's passing that it felt like the most profound kind of melancholy he could feel. To all his friends, he kept repeating:

"My heart is buried with that sweet girl."

Lincoln used to sit by his graveside and read the small, pocket-sized Testament that he carried around with him.

Lincoln felt the need to respond to all the rumors about him, even if they were false. In an open letter, he declared that he would not support any candidate for office if he knew that the person was a public enemy or a scoffer.

> *"Eternal consequences must be shared between each*
> *individual and his Divine Maker. Any man is not allowed to*
> *offend feelings or injure the morals of any other person. If*
> *Abe Lincoln, my guilt, should lead to me being held*
> *responsible for such conduct, I will not hold anyone*
> *accountable. But I will blame those who would falsely*
> *accuse of such conduct.*

Isaac Cogdal said that Lincoln had confessed to Ann Rutledge how much he loved her. He felt that she was his first love, and the first woman he loved so deeply and sacredly. She was a beautiful, intelligent girl who was an excellent wife. He could only think about her and how much he loved her.

Anne was charming, hardworking, and full of sweet spirit. Harvey Ross stated that she never sat still because she was so busy. She was always busy sewing for her family. Ann loved Abraham because she was passionate about a good education.

Herndon, Lincoln's law partner, said that he believed Abraham loved Ann Rutledge so much. He thought Lincoln's soul was so wrapped in Ann and that Ann was what most people considered to be the holiest thing in their lives. We know that this kind of love can never die.

Lincoln attempted to continue a courtship with Mary Owens a year after Rutledge's death.

Some historians claim that Mary Todd Lincoln was Lincoln's true love. Although this author cannot claim to be an expert historian or historian on Lincoln, his true interest in the lives and times of the Lincolns has prompted curiosity to find out everything that is available from reliable sources about the family and extended Lincoln families. All the research done on Lincoln and his lady friends has shown that Lincoln's true love was Ann Rutledge at sixteen. His true sexuality didn't blossom until later in life. It is strange that the depression that stayed with him throughout his entire life began after Ann's passing.

Mary Owens was his reason for being with Mary Owens. He wanted to see if Ann Rutledge could be gotten over.

Abraham Lincoln, 30 years old, tried to get up again at a cotillion and said so.

"Miss Mary Todd! I want to dance with your in the worst way."

Abraham called her the Edwards' house that evening. Abraham needed a wife to help him get into politics.

Mary Todd was a person who seemed to bring out his best qualities and lighten his mood. She was likely in a dark mood at the time of their split and he couldn't take it anymore.

Her family was not happy that she married Lincoln. Lincoln also felt that he wouldn't be able make her happy. Lincoln called it the "fatal January" when they got engaged in 1841.

It was not a real engagement, as we now call it. After a long period of relationship, Lincoln was back on business for several months. He knew that he needed to make amends with Mary and tell her that he wasn't interested in marriage. It was not a pretty breakup.

~

Abraham became depressed after the 'engagement' lasted 18 months.

~

It was quite shocking when Mary Lincoln and Abraham were suddenly married.

November 4, 1842. They were engaged to be married one day, and they were married the next day. Lincoln was caught up in an 'entanglement' with Mary and couldn't get out. He had to marry her. This was the only way to escape. Mary had purposely seduced Lincoln to trap him into marrying Mary.

~

Mary was 23 years old when they got married and Abraham was 33. Charles Dresser, an Episcopal minister, performed the ceremony.

~

Mary and Abraham were completely different. Mary was socially outgoing, chatty and enjoyed being surrounded by attention. Abraham, on the other hand, was quiet, solitary, and he preferred to be alone.

Mary was a spoilt young woman from the beginning until her marriage. Mary and Abraham rented a room above the Globe Tavern on Adams Street for $4 per week.

Mary was used to living in luxury and spaciousness, but she never complained about the discomfort of living in it compared to what she was able before she married.

The Lincolns soon discovered they were going to be parents. Their first child, Robert Todd Lincoln, was born August 1, 1843. Mary's father named him after him.

Robert's birth meant they needed more space. They moved to South Street, where they rented until Mary's father allowed them to purchase a house. Abraham's salary as a lawyer wasn't enough to buy a house.

Mary's father purchased their first house on the corner Eighth Street and Jackson Street in 1844. It had been owned by Minister Charles Dresser who was the minister who performed Mary's marriage to Abraham.

Add the months together and you'll see that Mary was either pregnant at the time Abraham married her, or that Robert was born two weeks earlier. It looks like he was born at 38 weeks, if you look at the 1842-1843 calendar. It shouldn't surprise you to learn about the history of Abrahams "supposed" sexual escapades and Marys "allegedly" sexual encounters.

Edward was their second child, born in 1846. They couldn't afford a maid because of the limited amount of money they had. Mary Todd Lincoln was forced to clean and cook for their home, care for their children and sew the clothes for them.

Lincoln, on the other hand, had his suits made and designed by Benjamin R. Biddle, a local tailor. Mary, who once had a positive disposition, became irritable after she changed her lifestyle. Abraham was also so involved with his job that he was out of town when he wasn't on the circuit.

Lincoln had "Mary & Abe – Love is Eternal" written on their wedding bands. To most outsiders, it seemed that their marriage was based on love. He said that Mary was just as beautiful as she was when she was a child, and that he was a poor man. But she fell in love with Lincoln and they never lost their love.

Everybody knows that the Lincoln marriage wasn't perfect. Mary and Abraham had their flaws. Mary was intelligent, creative, lively, cultured, witty and creative, but she was also selfish and anxious, nervous and irritable, which sometimes made her seem downright mean.

James Gourley, a Springfield neighbor of the Lincoln's, said that the Lincolns experienced their ups and downs like any family. Lincoln always gave in to Mary. Many men might have told their wives to stop whining or to shut up. Sometimes Abe would ignore Mary's hysterics, and sometimes he would laugh at Mary. Lincoln would take the children and pick Mary up if she continued her ranting and didn't calm down.

Mary's dual personality can be traced back her childhood. Mary's cousin stated that Mary was always high-strung and would laugh like mad and cry the next.

Staff at the White House noted that it was hard to be around her during her years. You would never know how she felt when you arrived at work each day.

She would be kind, thoughtful, kind, generous, considerate and hopeful one day and then be depressed the next.

~

Mary was known for her bad temper. This made her enemies. If she was offended, or angry in any way, her sweet ideas would vanish and her stinging terrible sarcastic voice or satirical voice will come out in bitterness.

~

John Nicolay and John Hay, White House secretaries, gave Mary the nickname "Hellcat," which means "she-wolf," and "female wildcat" because of their belief that Lincoln's terrible nature was responsible for a lifetime full of trouble and unhappiness. Some claim that she suffered from migraine headaches throughout her adult life, which caused her poor mood. Research suggests that she was a spoilt brat who became more spoiled as she grew older.

~

Elizabeth Keckly, Mary's seamstress had written 1868 that Lincoln was only an indulgent, kind husband. He would excuse Mary for any mistakes he saw in Mary, just as he would ignore the impulsive actions of a child.

~

Lincoln was, however, not the ideal husband. He seemed to be always away from Mary on the eighth circuit for six-eight month each year, leaving Mary with her children at home. Mary was terrified because she worried about house fires and burglaries, which scared her to death. Mary or Abraham would arrange for a neighbor boy to stay in Lincoln's home for Mary's protection.

Lincoln's political career began to flourish. He was often away from his family while giving speeches and attending rallies. Mary was not afraid of thunder and lightning, although she wasn't alone.

Mary was open about her disapproval of Lincoln's absence from the circuit. It seemed that he was the only circuit lawyer who was absent so much. Mary even said that Abraham Lincoln should stay home, and she would love him more if he did.

Mary complained even though he was at home. Lincoln was always busy with politics and work. He avoided social graces such as wearing the correct attire, inside or outside the house, and might even say inappropriate things out in public. He seemed to have no filter.

Lincoln didn't seem to respect Mary, the homemaker in their home. He would often arrive late at night or not at all for dinner. Mary didn't know he would bring friends to dinner. He never complimented her for the delicious food she made. Lincoln's marriage was plagued by problems, made worse by his terrible anger and Lincoln's withdrawal.

It is impossible to ignore the psychological impact Abraham Lincoln had upon his wife. His patience and love seemed to be the perfect hypnotics for Mary's erratic and violent temper.

Lincoln was once teased by someone about Mary's tantrums. He replied that it did not harm him and that it does her a lot good. This should keep you from ever having to wonder why I am so meek. Lincoln was not submissive but he was likely too indulgent, too parental, and too patient.

Mary was thrilled when Lincoln called Mary his "child-wife".

PART IV

THE LINCOLN BOYS

<<You cannot escape the responsibility of tomorrow by evading it today.>>

Abraham Lincoln and Mary Lincoln were blessed to have four boys.

Edward Baker Lincoln was just four years old when he died. This was about one month before his fourth birthday. According to census records, "chronic consumption" was the cause of death at that time. Today however, it is "tuberculosis". Multiple endocrine carcinoma or medullary thymic cancer is a type of hereditary cancer that many family members believe the features are compatible. This was also known as "consumption", which was used to describe any wasting disease. Eddie also had a thick, but lopsided lower lip which was a sign of the disease. The MEN2B gene is inherited by 100% of people who develop thyroid cancer. Sometimes it can appear as early as the newborn period.

In one of the White House guest rooms, was William Wallace Lincoln (Willie), an 11-year-old boy. He lay in what is now known as the Lincoln Bed. It is a large rosewood carved bed. At 5:00 p.m. on February 20, 1862, he had already died. He died of Typhoid fever, which he may have contracted from the contaminated water he drank at the White House.

Mary Todd Lincoln's seamstress Elizabeth Keckly was the one who dressed and cleaned him for his funeral. Abraham Lincoln would look at Willie and mourn the loss of his boy, who was too gifted for this world. He believed that

God had called him home. Lincoln believed Willie was better in heaven but they loved him so deeply. It was hard for him to leave.

Keckly observed Lincoln sink his head into his hands, and then his tall, lean frame erupt with sobs. Keckly sat at the foot of Lincoln's bed and watched as he moved. Keckly said that she will never forget those moments when the genius and greatness of the United States President were so intense. She wept over her child. Lincoln marched down the hall toward John Nicolay, who was in the White House. He told Nicolay that his boy was dead. Nicolay then recalled seeing Lincoln burst into tears, before he entered his office.

Mary Todd Lincoln was so ill that she couldn't console herself after the loss of Willie. Even worse, Tad, the third child born to the Lincolns on December 21st 1850, was in a different room at the White House. He had also died the year before.

According to one of the Government officials' wives, the White House felt sad because Willie seemed to have lost his joy and light. He was a brilliant child and precocious for his age. Everyone who knew him loved him. Mary stated that Willie was their "idolized" child.

They allowed Willie's corpse to be taken downstairs to the White House Green Room, where it remained until its time for burial. Alexander and Doctor Brown handled the embalming. This was the same procedure that would be done in three years for another death.

Willie was laid to rest in a coffin covered with flowers and made of metal so that it looked like rosewood. A silver plate had his name, birth date, and death inscribed. Friends came to pay their respects on February 24, the day of the funeral.

The Lincolns met around Willie's coffin before the service to say their last private farewells. Benjamin French was responsible for all arrangements. He said that the city was hit with one of the worst wind and rain storms in years. It felt like the storm was howling at Mrs. Lincoln. She was wrapped up in her grief, but not depressed. Mary Todd Lincoln stayed in bed grieving throughout the funeral and burial.

The funeral began at 2:20 p.m. in the White House East Room. There, the gilt mirrors were covered in mourning. Black fabric was used to cover the frames while white fabric was used for the glass. Willie's funeral was officiated by Dr. Gurley, New York Avenue Presbyterian Church. This church was home to the Lincoln family, which is why Willie told his Sunday School teacher that he would like to preach or teach the gospel.

After the service was over, many people followed the body from Georgetown to Oak Hill Cemetery in Georgetown. This made for a very long procession. Two white horses pulled a hearse and two black horses pulled a President's carriage up the hill towards the cemetery.

They placed Willie's body into the small chapel at the cemetery for a brief service of Scripture and prayer. Later, Willie would be moved into the vault of the Carroll Family in the northwest corner of the cemetery.

Willie's coffin, which had been moved in April 1865, was placed on a funeral train. It was then permanently placed in Oak Ridge Cemetery in Springfield.

Willie's death left deep, painful scars for the entire Lincoln family. Miss Keckly stated that Mary Todd Lincoln was not the same after Willie's death. She never entered the Guest Room again, and she never entered the Green Room to embalm her child.

On the day Lincoln was to be killed, he said to Mary that they should be more joyful because they were miserable after losing Willie and the war.

Tad, who was twelve years old when his father died, was the only child left with Mary. He was also the only one she could rely on for comfort. Mary wrote in November 1865, in one of her letters, that she could push Abraham Lincoln closer in her heart because she loved him so much.

Willie and Tad were both very inept at education. Tad was allowed to have fun and do what he wanted. This makes it difficult to understand why boys didn't get a good education from their father at an earlier age.

Mary finally enrolled Tad at a Racine school, Wisconsin, when the fall of 1865 arrived. Mary wrote Frances Carpenter in November, one of the painters who lived and worked in the White House while she painted the picture of Lincoln during the Emancipation Proclamation. She also revealed that Tad loved learning new things and was just as happy when he could play around in the White House.

Tad was sent to public school after Racine. He was only 13 years old at the time and couldn't read. His large stature probably caused him to be teased in school.

Remember that he had a speech impairment and was called "Stuttering Tad" by his classmates. His mother Mary Todd wasn't consistent in her parenting techniques. She wasn't lenient or strict about how she treated him. It was a confusing time for Tad.

In 1868, Robert Lincoln was 25 years old. He had decided to consult specialists about Tad's speech problems and some improvements seem to have been made.

Mary decided that she would move Tad and her family to Europe in the summer 1868. She felt Tad would be better educated there.

The government wasn't taking care of President's widows at the time. Now, our government is taking care of First Families. Mary Todd Lincoln visited Congress to plead for ex-presidents to be given to their widows.

According to the research, it would be fair to call it Mary throwing a fit with all the men in Congress. It must have worked, as Congress debated and began giving financial support to her and all widows of Presidents. They probably weren't happy to learn that she was sending Tad to Europe to get some education. Mary didn't care about it, and she and Tad set sail to Germany anyway.

Tad didn't know what was happening when he began the accelerated school in Germany. Mary thought Tad was improving in his studies. But by October that year, they had to move to England as Tad required a tutor for seven hours every day.

Mary fell ill during the first half of 1871. Tad started to feel symptoms. They returned to Chicago.

Mary was able to get better but Tad kept getting worse. Tad died on July 15, 1871, at the age of 18 years.

The Chicago Tribune published a notice about Tad's death on the following day. The notice stated that he died at the Clifton House where he was ill since returning from Europe. His cause of death was said to be chest dropsy. According to The Tribune, his symptoms began while he was abroad. After he returned to the States, his condition worsened. He then fell asleep during the night with very few clothes on. After a relapse, he began a slow decline.

It's not difficult to see that Eddy died at four years of age, Willie dying at five, and then President Lincoln and Tad, that Mary Todd Lincoln began her mental and emotional decline.

Robert Todd Lincoln was the oldest son. He was sometimes called "Prince Of Rails", but he hated his nicknames. As a child, he was cross-eyed, but as a teenager he became more reserved and determined.

He left his home at sixteen to go to Phillips Exeter School and Harvard University. Robert didn't like public life, but he did enjoy the attention that he received from the public. He was sometimes self-centered and vain at times. This made him distant from his family, and most importantly his father. As a child, he spent less time with his father than his brothers.

Robert was shy, kind, and reserved. He felt like he was always in the shadow of his father. Robert was a person everyone liked because he was honest and had good sense. This helped him win respect and goodwill in his personal life.

Robert became a prominent figure even while he was still a student during 1861-1865. He could not escape the media's attention.

Robert was in a difficult position due to his growing hatred of publicity. There was already a rumour that the son of the President was being formed. He was not snobbish, arrogant or able to keep his distance from the prying eyes of the public. But if he tried to profit off the position of being the son-in-law of a President, he would be condemned for it.

Robert was a young boy when his father was absent. Abe Lincoln would often be seen in circuit courts giving speeches or attending political rallies. Robert was sixteen years old when Abraham Lincoln became his father. Robert then went to New Hampshire, Harvard Law School, and by the time Abraham Lincoln was president, he had already graduated from Harvard Law School. Robert stated that his father was the president of the United States and Robert never spent more than ten minutes talking to him.

Robert resigned from Harvard Law School to serve as an officer in Grant's Army. He was criticised for not being serving in the Army.

Robert wanted to join the army earlier than he did. Mary Lincoln couldn't stand the idea of him joining, since he was her only child.

Abraham Lincoln said to Mary Todd Lincoln, "Many mothers have given up all their sons" and that our son is not more precious than those of other mothers.

Abraham Lincoln then told Mary that all men who love their country should be required by law to participate in the war effort. Mothers and fathers should be open-minded and not selfish about allowing their sons to serve.

Robert Todd Lincoln had breakfast with his family on the morning of President Lincoln's assassination. Robert and the President looked at a photograph and read the newspaper about General Robert E. Lee. Robert Todd Lincoln was told by Lincoln that he was happy that the war was over and that Robert was safely home. Robert was told by Lincoln that he wanted to trade in his uniform, return to college and complete his three-years of studies. By the end of this time, he would know if he would make a good attorney.

Lincoln was happier than he'd been in a long time. Robert, Lincoln's oldest child, died in 1926 at the age 82.

One thing is certain: Abe Lincoln and Mary Lincoln shared a mutual love and interest in all their boys' activities and, more importantly, their boys' welfare.

Lincolns had their quarrels and at times they got quite hectic. They were often exaggerated by the wagging of tongues.

Mary was prone to temper tantrums, frequent headaches, and a horrible sense of insecurity and loneliness.

PART V

THE MADNESS OF MARY LINCOLN

<<Whatever you are, be a good one.>>

Abraham Lincoln

Mary Lincoln's problems didn't start when she married Abraham Lincoln. They started as a child who was very spoiled and refused to be governed. She would have temper tantrums until someone gave in and allowed her to have her way.

Many books don't have enough space to talk about Mary Lincoln's madness and her bizarre ways. Mary was the center of attention, and many tongues loved to wag.

Both Mary and Abraham had psychological injuries that could have crippled them emotionally. This might have led to the problems they would face as husband and wife.

Mary's family, The Edwards, lived in Springfield just down the street from Mary Lincoln and Abe Lincoln. Mary was a popular young woman among Springfield's young men and was often courted by aspiring lawyers and politicians. Mary was intelligent, clever, smart, graceful, and great at entertaining and talking.

Mary is about 130 pounds in weight and average height. Her face was round, her hair was dark brown, and her eyes were blue-gray. She was proud, vivacious and quite pretty.

Mary was quick-witted and could judge the intentions of everyone. Although she was charming most of the time, her manners were very charming. However, if she ever offends you, she can eat your liver by being sarcastic or bitter. She was very different from Lincoln in terms of her height, temperament and education.

Abraham Lincoln was in Springfield when he chased Matilda Edwards, a teenager. All the men in town noticed Matilda in 1841.

Matilda Edwards is believed to have broken more male hearts than any other Springfield girl. Matilda believed that men would like her if they didn't.

It is said that Todd was a sexy woman who had many suitors but it was not clear that she pursued Lincoln. Orville Browning, another attorney, believed that Mary Todd was responsible for all the chasing after Lincoln. It was revealed that Lincoln had admitted to Mary Todd, in all of the conversations, that he was in love with Matilda Edwards.

Mary Todd appeared to be eager to marry Lincoln. Lincoln seemed to believe that "marital bliss" was an exaggeration.

Lincoln pardoned a soldier who was leaving home to marry his love. Lincoln signed all necessary documents and told the intercessor that he wasn't punishing the soldier because he knew he would regret it in less than twelve month. Many evidence supports the idea that Lincoln disliked his marriage just as much as he thought his soldier would.

Although there were always visitors to the White House, one visitor was particularly notable from New York. Because of his reputation, no woman with a good reputation should ever see him. He had been to Europe and no one knows where he got the money. He was very attentive to Mrs. Lincoln and Mr. Lincoln, but more to Mary Todd Lincoln.

He was so often at the White House that all of President Obama's friends noticed it. He was always the first to arrive at Mary Lincoln's reception. He would always show up at any informal dinner. He would show up even though everyone else was gone. He was always seen by the White House servants.

Wycliffe was heard complimenting Mary Todd Lincoln's appearance and dressing in such a way that most men would be embarrassed to approach her. Instead, she accepted Wikoff as her guide in social etiquette and personal requirements. She also welcomed visitors to her salon on drives and in other domestic arrangements.

He was seen more than once riding in the Presidential coach with women along Pennsylvania Avenue. He didn't try to conceal his presence. It was not appropriate or complimenting for the President's family. It was made scandalous by some papers.

Wikoff was treated with contempt and this was widespread. As Wikoff sat on a bench in President's Park one September, others were listening to Marine Band Music. If you look up at the Grand Portico of the White House one last time, Mary Todd Lincoln was there, and Wikoff was nowhere else.

Mary Todd Lincoln was a very vain woman. She wore her dresses with more coverage at the top to show off her breasts, and had a longer train than any fashion required. She was proud of her neck and bust, which bothered President Lincoln.

Edwin Emery, a historian, noted that parts of Abraham Lincoln's first speech to Congress in December 1861 appeared suddenly in the Herald newspaper on the morning Lincoln was to deliver his talk.

John Hickman, Chair of the House Judiciary Committee, turned it into an investigation to find out where the leak started. The leak was traced to Wikoff, and the sordid scene was covered up before the facts became public.

Many believed that Wikoff had obtained the speech from Mary Todd Lincoln. Wikoff was taken into custody and Sickles made a deal to get John Watt, the

White House Gardner, to confess to having memorized the message when he saw it at the President's home office.

It was eventually discovered that Lincoln was wanted out by a group of New Yorkers, so they hired an impoverished man to serve their purposes. He was given the instructions and the money to do his horrible deeds by a couple. He was to get inside the White House and flatter the women. Wikoff would regularly send brief bulletins to his New York bosses, letting them know how he was doing.

Robert Lincoln was always the one who was pushed to the side, but he was the one that ended up saving the family. Robert tried to claim it began July 2, 1863 with a carriage accident. While riding towards Washington from Soldier's Home, the driver's seat of the carriage fell apart, throwing the driver to the ground.

Mary leapt from her carriage to save herself after the horses became scared and began running along Rock Creek Road in panic.

According to the accident report, Mary was bruised, shocked, and battered. However, there were no broken bones and her injuries didn't seem to be life-threatening. A sharp stone had caused a cut to her back. Robert, a student at Cambridge, received a telegraph from President Lincoln. He told him to relax and that his mother was only slightly hurt by her fall.

Along with the physical injuries, there were also emotional consequences.

Mary's nurse thought the accident was an attempt to assassinate the President. The driver's seat had been sabotage. Mary was even more worried about her husband's safety.

Because he was so busy with war management, the President didn't have much time for Mary. Robert was sure that he didn't see his mom, and decided to ignore his dad's telegrams. Mary felt more distant from her family because she had Tad to give her her undivided attention.

Mary went to bed. President Lincoln hired Rebecca Pomroy again, the nurse who cared for Mary after Willie's and Tad's deaths. Mary's benign wound got infected. Mary was finally able to get out of bed after three weeks.

Mary suffered from migraines her whole life. It seemed that the headaches were getting worse after the accident.

Robert Lincoln shared later with his aunt that his mother had not fully recovered from her head injury. He felt that it had an effect on her mental health.

Mary's intense grief over Willie's passing, along with the side effects of her head injury didn't make her crazy, but it did bring her closer to the edge. Mary's half-sister Emily Helm noticed in 1863 that Mary was anxious, exaggerated, and always afraid of what bad things might happen.

Emily also wrote in her diary about a night Mary came to her bedroom smiling, with her eyes brimming and saying that Willie had visited her that night. He comes to my bedroom every night and stands at the foot of mine. Eddie is sometimes with him, but he doesn't always come by himself. Emily told her that seeing him brought her great comfort.

It is impossible to know, but it could have been Mary experiencing psychotic symptoms. Mary would sleep on one side of her bed in her later years, so Lincoln could rest on the other.

Despite having Robert in her entire life, she decided to put Robert's name in the newspaper. This gave her some relief from the pain of losing her son, and also her place in society.

Abraham and Mary seemed to have drifted apart from 1863 to Lincoln's death. Because she was afraid that he would bring up topics like her extravagant spending or all her debts, she stayed away. Because he was not confident in her judgement, mental health, and the people she might tell, he never confided in her. Mary was not the right person to share sensitive information with. They had little to talk about.

Orville H. Browning, Lincoln's friend, said that Mr. Lincoln once told him that he was worried about Mary's disgrace and that he would be unable to remember the details. He was always on guard for Mary's jealousy of his conversations with other women.

Mary seemed to have tested and strengthened the President's inborn qualities of patience, tolerance, and perseverance during their later marriage years.

In 1875, she was officially diagnosed as insane. Mary was always very emotional and Willie's death left her devastated. Mary hid in her room for several weeks. This caused Robert Lincoln and Elizabeth to ask Mary Todd, Elizabeth's older sister to visit Mary at the White House.

Mary couldn't look at Willie's things. After two months, Aunt Elizabeth moved on and President Lincoln hired a nurse. Mary got rid all Willie's clothes and possessions. She also made sure that none of Willie or Tad's friends (mainly Holly and Bud Taft) were allowed to visit the White House.

Mary was forced to wear what they called "widows weeds" after Abraham Lincoln died. But before that, she had a huge collection of costly gowns that would never be worn again. She decided to sell some of her exquisite dresses in order to raise funds.

Before the Smithsonian Institute launched the First Ladies Collection, it all happened. Mary Todd Lincoln traveled to New York using an assumed name. Elizabeth Keckley, her dressmaker, was also with her. They searched for buyers in thrift shops and resale shops. They were not willing to spend the amount she requested for the dresses.

Mary Todd Lincoln was entangled in a dubious pair of salespeople who sold her a poor bill of goods. They knew Mary and convinced her to sell the dresses at an auction. Mary took the bait.

The situation became more complicated and Mary Lincoln returned to Chicago, leaving Lizzie Keckley as the sales manager. Mary Lincoln was tricked by the auctioneers into giving them what they called "personal letters" that they could show any potential buyer. It was more blackmail than glitter.

Mary's dress auction became a huge scandal that was widely reported in the media. Even worse, Mary had to pay more than $800 for her dresses to be returned.

Mary Lincoln was predisposed to psychiatric illness and had suffered from emotional and mental trauma throughout her life. She was eventually committed to an insane asylum. Mary was diagnosed by a psychiatrist with bipolar disorder.

Mary could have had many different reasons for her bizarre behavior and declining mental health. Mary Todd Lincoln could have encouraged President Lincoln to stay home that evening. Mary's life, and many others, might have been different. It is sad but true that Mary held Lincoln's hand at the time he was killed. While I can't be certain about any other author, it is enough for me to say that this author would be insane without question.

Abraham Lincoln knew what to do to help Mary with her mental problems. He seemed to know exactly what to do and how best to calm her down each time.

Mary was made Robert's responsibility after the death of Lincoln. It is well documented how he treated Mary, the reasons he had her committed, his response to her suicide attempt, and even how Mary plotted to kill Robert. Robert was not a bad boy. Eight months before her release, he agreed to let her out of the Psych Hospital.

Robert was living in Chicago when the Hotel called him and asked him to come get his mother, who was still naked in the Hotel lobby.

Mary was so bad at spending that she would spend money even if there wasn't any. Mary would have the White House bookkeepers juggle her books and lie to Lincoln about how much she was spending.

Another explanation is available, one that her doctors tried to conceal for as long as they could. It was possible that Mary and President had both syphilis. Mary's delusions may have been caused by nerve cells that were no longer carrying information to her brain. All of it was caused by syphilis. Mary was suffering from all the symptoms of syphilis, including weight loss, dementia, severe back pain and impaired coordination.

Lincoln's Springfield law partner, William Herndon, told the story of syphilis. He wrote in his private notes that Lincoln went to Beardstown in 1835-36 and, while there, became involved in a passionate moment with the disease.

Mary Lincoln died on July 16th 1882 from what was believed to be a stroke. An autopsy revealed that she also had a brain tumour. It was unknown what kind of brain tumor it was, or how long it had been growing. This could have explained her mood swings or eccentricities.

Mary became almost blind as she grew older and lost a lot weight. It was possible that she had diabetes. We don't know if the blindness was due to diabetes, cataracts or syphilis.

PART VI

QUESTIONABLE RUMORS ABOUT LINCOLN

<<You can fool all the people some of the time, and some of the people all the time, but you cannot fool all the people all the time.>>

Abraham Lincoln

Everyone knew of the rumors that Lincoln, a young man from Springfield, Illinois, shared a bed with Joshua Speed for four years. Speed was perhaps Lincoln's closest friend.

When you read the letters between Speed and Lincoln after Speed left Kentucky for marriage, it was clear that he was still having an affair with Joshua Speed. Lincoln was also nervous about Mary Todd's wedding in Springfield. Both were anxious about the wedding night.

This book will not contain any information about Lincoln or Speed's relationship after their marriage. Lincoln was 28 years old when he was admitted to the bar. He moved from New Salem, Massachusetts to Springfield which seemed like a large metropolis of '1500' people. Lincoln arrived in Springfield in spring 1837. He immediately went to the General Store to find out how much it would cost to sleep on a mattress and some sheets. He could only afford that amount and would have to share his bed with another man. Joshua Speed was a man he'd never met before.

It was clear that Springfield, Illinois residents didn't like to talk about Lincoln. Although they did not intend to tell good things about Lincoln, they would be able to reveal his weaknesses if forced to. They would gladly reveal all of

Lincoln's weaknesses and damaging facts that they witnessed every day. The people of Springfield seem to have hated him in secret.

Henry Whitney, a fellow lawyer, felt Lincoln was constantly courting him. He said that Lincoln had told him to have sexual contact because it was like having a thousand strings.

Lincoln could have meant it in many different ways. This could have been referring to a woman. If we don't get the whole conversation, this statement may have been misinterpreted.

Henry Whitney is known for making stories more interesting and stretching the truth. This means that no matter who the tidbit is from, it doesn't necessarily mean it is true.

Many people want to know the details of how these contacts were made. One Billy Greene, a grammar teacher who lived with Lincoln in New Salem around 1831, gave a hint.

Greene described Lincoln as an influential figure and said that he found Lincoln attractive. He also commented on Lincoln's strong thighs. Femoral intercourse was a form of orgasm that was mutually beneficial and was usually between the firm thighs of the other?

There are many evidence to suggest that the 'affair' began in September.

8th of August 1862: President would visit the Soldier's Home (as always when Mrs. Lincoln would travel to New York for serious shopping).

Lincoln sent Captain David Derickson to get to know him. Derickson was five feet nine inches tall, with deep set eyes and thick black hair. Derickson was nine years younger than Lincoln at the time he was born. He was 44 years old when the affair began. He had nine children from two wives. One of his grown children served with Company K.

Lincoln did also visit Springfield's whorehouse, which charged three dollars. Lincoln didn't have the money and asked for credit. The girl eventually gave it to Lincoln for free.

It is hard to believe how many times syphilis has been spread. Lincoln believed he was being treated. However, at the time, there wasn't any real treatment for syphilis. They didn't know how the virus could travel to the brain.

If Lincoln was to rise in Illinois' political world, it would be necessary that he take a wife and start a family. He ended the engagement. He went to bed after the split. He wrote a poem he called "Suicide" that was published in Springfield's local newspaper. The file copy was then secretly deleted.

The truth about Lincoln's sexual orientation remains to be established. Each person who reads this book will have to make their own decision.

As a final note, I'd like to add: Nothing new has happened under the sun. Also, it doesn't matter how old the century is, there has never been anything like it before.

No matter how beautiful a house or the color of a front door, nobody can know what's going on behind it.

PART VII

RACING TOWARDS POLITICS

<<Nearly all men can stand adversity, but if you want to test a man's character, give him power.>>

Abraham Lincoln

Lincoln was an early adopter of freethinking and skeptical thinking. Lincoln felt his reputation was tarnished because he complained once about the 'church influence' that was used when he entered politics.

Lincoln ran for Congress in 1846. He had handbills printed that denied that he ever had any disrespectful remarks about religion. However, he didn't stop there. He continued to state that he believed in a doctrine called necessity.

"The human mind is always compelled to act or held back by another power over something the mind cannot control."

Lincoln believed in dreams, omens, and enigmatic signs throughout his life. As he grew up and faced all the responsibilities of being president, Lincoln seemed to have a deeper sense of religion. He was able to express his belief in the necessity of God.

He began to see himself as an 'instrument for Providence' and to view all of the ancient time as the work of God.

Lincoln said in 1862 that God could have a purpose for the Civil War. However, it was possible that God may have a different purpose than what each side is fighting for. The individual objectives that work are one of God's best ways to accomplish His purpose.

Lincoln loved the Bible. He knew the Bible well. There are other researchers who will tell you that Lincoln wasn't a big believer in the Bible.

Lincoln loved Shakespeare as well. In private conversations, he would often use Shakespearean references to discuss the dramaturgical interpretations with considerable insight. He would also recite long passages from memory with rare feelings and understanding.

Andrew Jackson was the U.S. president when Lincoln entered politics for the first time. Lincoln supported Jackson's ideas for common men, but was not in agreement with their views on how the government should separate from the economic enterprise.

Lincoln stated later that he would do for the people what they were unable to do in their individual capacities, but that he would be able to legitimize the government whenever it was necessary.

Henry Clay and Daniel Webster were two prominent politicians at that time, which Lincoln loved the most. Both politicians advocated using the federal government's power to encourage business and develop America's resources. This included a protective tariff, an internal improvement program for external transportation improvements and the use of the national bank. Lincoln believed that Illinois and the West needed economic development aid, and he began to associate with the Whigs (the party of Webster, Clay) from the beginning.

Lincoln was a member the Illinois Legislature, for which he was elected four times, beginning in 1834 and ending with 1840. It was Lincoln who started putting his efforts into big projects that were constructed with state funds. These included highways, canals, and a network of railroads and other infrastructure.

Both the Democrats and the Whigs voted for an Omnibus Bill to cover all these developments. However, the panic of 1837 combined with the economic depression caused the collapse of most businesses. While he was still in the legislature, it was clear that he opposed slavery and was not an abolitionist.

In 1837, there was the murder by a mob of Elijah Lovejoy. He was against slavery and was a reporter for Alton's newspaper. The Illinois legislature passed resolutions condemning abolitionist societies. They also defended slavery's position in all southern states under the Federal Constitution. Lincoln refused to vote against the recommendations.

Lincoln and another congressman wrote a protest that said, on one hand, slavery was founded on injustice and poor policy, and on the other, it was also based on the endorsement by the abolition doctrines, which tend to increase rather than decrease the evils.

Lincoln was the only Whig in Illinois during his term (1847-1849) and was not paying much attention to the legislative issues. One bill was proposed by Lincoln for the gradual and reimbursed liberation of slaves in the District of Columbia. It was only to take effect with approval from 'free white citizens' who lived in the district. This drove the abolitionists insane, and slaveholders were never seriously considered.

Lincoln spent a lot of time during this period focusing on getting elected president. During the Mexican War, he had only found one issue and one candidate. Lincoln called his "spot resolutions" and argued with President Polk's statement that Mexico was the one who started the whole war by spreading American blood across American soil. Lincoln, along with other Whig party members, was able to criticize Polk and the entire war effort and vote to continue it. He was working for the nomination and getting Zachary Taylor elected war hero.

Lincoln thought he would be the commissioner of the general land office after Taylor's victory in election polls. He was rewarded for his services during his campaign and he was certain that he would get the job. However, he was not able to get the job he had hoped for.

He was critical of the war and not popular among his district's voters. He was 40 years old and was unhappy with politics. It looked as if he was near the end of his political career.

PART VIII

ON THE ROAD TO THE PRESIDENCY

<<Give me six hours to chop down a tree and I will spend the first four sharpening the axe.>>

Abraham Lincoln

~

Lincoln would not be able to take part in politics again for at least five years, and it was only then that a new crisis prompted him to return to politics and to rise to the level of statesmanship.

~

Stephen Douglas, one Lincoln's rivals, introduced to Congress in 1854 a bill that would open the entire Louisiana Purchase to slavery. It would also allow Nebraskans and Kansasans to decide for themselves whether or not to allow slaveholding in the territory.

~

The Nebraska-Kansas Act provoked violent opposition in Illinois and other states in the Northwest. It created the Republican Party as the Whig Party was moving towards its disintegration.

Lincoln, like many homeless Whigs, was soon to become a Republican. Not long after, prominent Republicans in the East tried to recruit Douglas to the Republican camp. They also attempted to pull Douglas' Democratic group to West. Lincoln stated that he would not be part of the effort. Lincoln was the one who was determined that Douglas should not be the Republican in charge of his state.

When 1858 arrived, Lincoln challenged Stephen Douglas to the Senate seat. Then the debates began and they continued throughout Illinois, making history that will never be forgotten.

Although both men were great debaters and excellent stump speakers, they were completely different in their appearances and dressing. Douglas, a plump and short man with a strong voice and graceful gestures that easily won over his audience, was plump but not as tall.

You then had Lincoln, a tall, stocky, and anorexic-looking man who moved awkwardly and had a shrill, piercing voice. Lincoln's speeches and prose were clear, concise, without wordiness and as compelling as they sound.

When you looked at the situation objectively, Douglas and Lincoln weren't that different when it was time to argue over politics.

They had the same views about proslavery, and abolition. Lincoln, and not Douglas, insisted that slavery be banned in the territories.

Douglas disagreed with Lincoln. He believed that the territories were not suitable for slavery and Congress did not have the legislation necessary to stop slavery spreading.

Lincoln made a famous speech in which he stated that

"A house divided against itself cannot stand."

Lincoln believed that the government couldn't be permanently freed from slavery and could not remain in a state where half of its citizens were slaves. He predicted at that time that the country would become either all slaves or all non-slave.

Lincoln stated that he would insist on civil liberties for every American citizen, regardless of race or color, because all were at stake.

He would assure his viewers, depending on their audience at the time, that he would not allow citizenship for black people or believe in equality for all races.

He told a Charleston crowd that he was against making blacks voters or jurors and that he would not allow them to hold office or marry whites. Lincoln said that the physical differences between the races would forever be a problem for the two tracks who lived together in terms of social and political equality.

Douglas lost the election to Lincoln in the end. Lincoln was not surprised by the outcome, but it did cause him to fall into deep depression. It was clear that Lincoln's victory had put him in the national spotlight. Soon, people were talking about Lincoln running for president in the 1860 elections.

Lincoln was known to have worn a stovepipe cap because it was his favorite style of hat. It was much more than just a hat for Lincoln. Lincoln used it as his portable filing cabinet, where he kept all his notes and letters.

May 18th, 1861 Lincoln was nominated by the Republican Convention in Chicago. He quit his law practice and stopped making stump speeches, giving his full attention to his presidential campaign.

Lincoln worked with a united Republican party, while the Democrats had four candidates. Lincoln won the election on November 6th. Lincoln received no votes in the Deep South, and in the whole country, he got 40 percent of the 100 votes. He was able win a clear majority of popular votes thanks to the distribution of them.

Mary believed she was a hotshot when Lincoln was president. She had truly reached her destiny.

South Carolina resigned from the Union after Lincoln was elected, but before he was inaugurated. To prevent other Southern states from making this same mistake, there were several compromises made in Congress. The most important was the Crittenden Compromise.

Before Mary Todd, Abraham Lincoln and their new White House home were even completed, they faced a crisis that six other states had already experienced.

South Carolina had withdrawn from the Union and formed the Confederate States of America. Things were already as bad as they could be.

Both the North and South began to focus on Fort Sumter in Charleston Harbor, South Carolina. While the fort was still being constructed, it was occupied by U.S. troops, under Major Robert Anderson's supervision. It was immediately claimed by the Confederacy. Lincoln recognized trouble in Springfield immediately and requested Winfield Scott, the general-in-chief for the U.S. Army, to assist him. Scott instructed them to prepare to retake the forts or to hold them as the case may require.

Lincoln was barely in office when he heard that Fort Sumter would not be withdrawn or supplied if it wasn't. Scott and others tried to persuade Lincoln to leave Fort Sumter.

On the other side, many Republicans felt that if they showed weakness, it could spell disaster for the Republican Party as well as the Union.

Lincoln ordered two expeditions for Fort Pickens, and one for Fort Sumter. Lincoln had already sent someone to South Carolina as a messenger before the Sumter expedition. He wanted to inform the governor that the Confederates would present Major Anderson with a demand for Fort Sumter's evacuation and would not wait for Lincoln's arrival. On April 12, 1861, Confederates began firing in the harbor at dawn. The Civil War was already underway.

Lincoln told Congress that those who were attacking the government had started their conflict towards them when they met July 4th. Confederates then accused Lincoln of being an aggressor. Confederates claimed that Lincoln was intelligent in the way he maneuvered them to fire their first shot, so they would have been the ones who started war. These facts are believed to be distorted by some historians. Lincoln was determined to preserve the Union. However, he needed to maintain the Union and stand against the South in order to do so. Lincoln decided to take Fort Sumter as his greatest stand.

Lincoln believed that the war would end in a brief one when it began. Lincoln requested that the governors of the states send troops to Fort Sumter after the first shots were fired. Virginia, along with three other states in the upper South, responded by joining the Confederacy.

Then he blocked all Southern ports. These were the first decisions Lincoln made as commander in chief of the U.S. Navy & Army. Lincoln wanted a plan that included a command system for carrying out all this.

General Scott advised Lincoln to not go to war with Confederate troops.

Virginia, so that he could control the Mississippi River and tighten his blockade to hold the South with a huge crush.

Lincoln appeared to doubt Scott's plan that was Anaconda-like. He believed that war must be aggressive to win it.

Lincoln's closest assistants would have told you that the White House on the Potomac at the time was not the best place. The stench from the Potomac wafting from death was nauseating and stayed with you day and night. It was impossible to escape it. It was made worse by the summer heat, which forced the White House to open its windows because of the heat.

Lincoln believed he had everything under his control. Lincoln was aware that so many people hated and had lost two of their children. He also lost his love. He saw death every day from his front yard at the white house. It is impossible to feel down?

Scott was overthrown by Lincoln who ordered a full-on advance on the Virginia front. This resulted in the defeat of the federal forces at Bull Run on the 21st of July 1861.

Lincoln issued memos detailing their military strategy after many nights of sleepless nights. Lincoln believed that the armies had to move in a parallel pattern on multiple fronts. He also thought it was necessary to use the support of Unionists in Kentucky and eastern Tennessee, western Virginia and Missouri.

It was the core of Lincoln's strategy, along with the naval blockade. Lincoln was a war leader and used the same style as a politician, describing himself in a way he never regretted.

Lincoln preferred to react to problems created by others than to create new policies or try to plan the long-term. Lincoln will admit that he didn't claim to have any control over events, but that certain events did influence him.

Lincoln was a pragmatic man. He was flexible and agile mentally. If one decision or action was not satisfactory in practice, he would work with another.

Lincoln would not hesitate to impose any of his ideas upon any of his generals but he would also experiment on his command troops and the whole organization. Lincoln accepted Scott's resignation and decided to give George McClellan command of all armies.

Lincoln was getting fed up with McClellan's slow pace after a few months and decided to degrade McClellan so that he could only command the Army of the Potomac. He began to wonder about the plans McClellan had for the Peninsular Campaign.

So they were able to capture Richmond, Virginia after the Seven Days' Battles

It failed from June 25th to July 1st 1862 and Lincoln ordered them to be disbanded. Lincoln tried again with a succession of Virginian commanders - John Pope and Ambrose Burnside, George Meade and Joseph Hooker - but they failed to impress him. McClellan was even more disappointed. As time passed, Lincoln was disappointed with each one of them.

Lincoln appointed Henry Halleck as general in chief. He would provide advice and be the intermediary between the field officers, but he didn't like making crucial decisions.

The Federal armies didn't have unity of command for nearly two years. General Halleck, President Lincoln and War Secretary Edwin Stanton acted as informal councils of war.

Lincoln would send his official orders through Halleck, communicate with his generals directly, and send his personal ideas in his name. Lincoln would suggest to any generals opposing Robert E. Lee that the object be to destroy Lee's army and drive the invader from Northern soil, not to capture Richmond.

Lincoln decided to look West for a leader General. Lincoln had always admired Ulysses Grant's leadership abilities in Mississippi.

Nine days had passed since Vicksburg surrendered to the United States on July 4, 1863, when Lincoln sent a "Thank You" note to express his gratitude for his valuable service.

Lincoln admitted to Grant in a note that he made an error. Grant was told by Lincoln that Grant had mistakenly thought Grant would bypass Vicksburg, instead of crossing the Mississippi and turning back to head toward Vicksburg. This would allow them to approach Vicksburg from behind.

Lincoln promoted Grant to lieutenant-general in March 1864, allowing him commands over all federal armies. Lincoln finally found someone with subordinates such as George H. and Philip Sheridan.

Thomas and William T. Sherman were able to make Lincoln's idea come to life on a large scale and coordinate the offensive that had to be carried out.

Lincoln, writing to Joshua Speed in 1855, was recalling a steamboat ride he and Speed had shared 14 years earlier on the Ohio River. Joshua Speed asked him if he had ever remembered that while riding down from Louisville, Kentucky to the Ohio River, there were ten to twelve slaves on board, all of them shackled together using irons. Lincoln stated that he was tormented by the sight when he first saw it.

Lincoln initially resisted the idea of abolitionist policies. There were many reasons he was hesitant at first. He was elected on a platform which promised no interference in slavery in the US.

Lincoln was also concerned about the difficulties of integrating almost four million blacks into American politics and society.

Lincoln rescinded the declaration made by Generals John C. Fremont and David Hunter, who sent it from their military units.

Congress passed the confiscation acts of 1861 and 1862, and Lincoln kept from fully enforcing the provisions that authorized him to start seizing slave property.

Due to the response toward the antislavery sentiment, Lincoln decided to come forward with his plan about emancipation. He proposed that the slaves would be freed by the action of the state, then the slaveholders would be reimbursed, and then the federal government would help in sharing the financial burden. The process of emancipation would be gradual; the men to be freed would be colonized abroad.

Congress agreed it was willing to vote that it would give the funds necessary toward the Lincoln plan, but there were none of the neighboring slave states that wanted to participate, and in any case, there were few African Americans who were in a leadership position that wanted to see their people sent abroad.

Lincoln wanted his original plan to be a success, but he issued a final Emancipation Proclamation on January 1, 1863. It decreed that only those sections of the country that were under Confederate control, and not to the slave states that were remaining loyal or to the occupied areas of the Confederacy.

Whether indirectly or directly this proclamation did bring freedom while the war was going on to less than 200,000 slaves. It was a substantial significant symbol. It also showed that Lincoln's government added freedom to the reunion as far as a war aim, and this attracted the liberal opinion in Europe and England for increased support in the Union cause.

Lincoln himself was not sure if the step he had decided to use was constitutional, except for use as a temporary measure during the war. Once the war was over, the slaves were all given their freedom by this proclamation but would have run the risk of being re-enslaved and had nothing else that was done in confirming their liberty.

So, there was something else done by way of the Thirteenth Amendment that was added to the Constitution, but Lincoln played his part in bringing to the country his change with the fundamental law.

By the chair of the Republican National Committee Lincoln urged the Republicans to start including a plank for amendments with its platform of 1864.

The plank as adopted, said that slavery had been the reason for the rebellion and that the President's Proclamation aimed a *"blow of death toward the large evil,"* and a constitutional amendment to be able to *"terminate and prohibit forever."*

At the time Lincoln was re-elected, the Republican majority held in Congress increased, Lincoln felt justified, and he had a mandate coming from the people for the Thirteenth Amendment.

For the new Congress that was chosen, it was mostly a Republican majority, would not meet until the lame duck session of the past Congress during winter 1864-65. Lincoln would not wait.

With Lincoln's resources for persuasion and patronage with certain Democrats, he got the necessary two-thirds vote before the session would end. He celebrated as the amendment was sent out to all the states for possible ratification, and he celebrated once more when Illinois first led and others states joined one by one to act favorably with it. Lincoln never lived to rejoice in its adoption.

People felt that Lincoln deserved his reputation he had earned as the Great Emancipator. Lincoln strengthened with the practical demonstrations where he gave respect for the dignity and human worth no matter the color of skin.

For Lincoln's last two years of living, he more than welcomed the African Americans as his friends and visitors in such a way as no president had ever done before. If there was a reception in the White House, African Americans were just as welcome to come through as whites and allowed to shake Lincoln's hands. To this Mary, Lincoln was having fits as they were messing up her carpets. Lincoln did not care. The carpets belonged to the people.

PART IX

WARTIME POLITICS

«I am not bound to win, but I am bound to be true. I am not bound to succeed, but I am bound to live by the light that I have. I must stand with anybody that stands right, and stand with him while he is right, and part with him when he goes wrong.»

Abraham Lincoln

If Lincoln were to win the war, he needed popular support. It seemed for the Union that Lincoln was the President that possessed that rare political skill of appealing to other fellow politicians. He had a way about him that would smooth over their differences and still hold on to the loyalty of the men who were antagonistic with one another.

However, the opposing party was alive, well, and secure. It consisted of a membership that held the '***War Democrats***' and the '***Peace Democrats***' who were sometimes called the '***Copperheads***,' and there were even some of them who would collaborate with the enemy.

After the war, Lincoln had to make a lot of hard decisions, and he justified his actions for the reasoning that one had to allow some sacrifices and parts of the country's Constitution.

Lincoln had a friend by the name of Orville H. Browning that felt the arrests that had been ordered by Lincoln were **'*arbitrary and illegal*,'** but were probably doing more harm than they were doing any good, causing more weakness instead of strengthening the U.S. Government. Still, Lincoln stood firm and defended his actions. He argued that the Constitution gave the reasoning for suspending the liberties '**in instances of an Invasion or a Rebellion, when the people's safety may be at risk**.'

Lincoln had inside his very own party, those who were confronting some of the factional divisions and their conflicts that were causing him nothing but trouble just like the Democrats. It was true that when it came to the economic plans that Lincoln and most of his Republican party agreed.

With Lincoln approving, the Republicans put into place a law that the essentials were things he had promoted from earlier in his political career like a national banking system, construction of a railroad to reach the Pacific Coast, a protective tariff, and use of federal aid for improvements internally for the United States.

Within the Republican Party, there were still two factions: The '**Conservatives**' and the '**Radicals**.' Lincoln leaned toward the Conservatives, but some of his friends were hanging out in the Radical section. It made it hard for Lincoln, but he had to work hard to maintain control and leadership over both sides.

When Lincoln appointed his cabinet, he chose those who believed as he did and those who were direct rivals for his 1860 nomination. He felt that it would give fair representation for each critical party.

It sounds like an uphill battle when you realize he included Seward who was an outstanding Conservative, and Salmon Chase was a die-hard Radical. Lincoln was quick like a fox and was able to quickly pull his cabinet through crises and managed to keep the opposites held together until Chase finally resigned in 1864.

Everyday Lincoln was dealing with more big issues such as factional uprisings breaking out in Congress. It seemed the most substantial issues were when it came to 'reconstructing' the South. The states of Arkansas, Tennessee, and Louisiana had pretty much already been recovered by the government's armies. It was late in 1863 when Lincoln decided to introduce his 10% plan. It would acknowledge that when a new state government would form that 10% of the voters who qualified had taken their oath for future loyalty toward the United States.

Of course, the Radical section rejected Lincoln's proposal were way too lenient, so they passed it through Congress by attaching it to the Wade-Davis Bill. That way they could have let the readmission and remaking of each state after there had been a majority had taken their loyalty oath. Lincoln then pocket-vetoed the bill; all its authors later published a 'manifesto' so they could denounce him.

Since Lincoln was already considered the candidate for the Republican party to be re-elected for President, with the Wade-Davis Manifesto, it signaled to the movement inside the party to get rid of Lincoln as the Republican's nominee. Lincoln was waiting patiently, not saying anything and hoping the action that was planned would collapse; but then when it happened, the party was more divided than ever.

There was a rival Republican candidate by the name of John C. Fremont, who was nominated a lot earlier by some splinter group out in the field. There were the leading Radicals that promised to get their hands on Fremont to withdraw if Lincoln would get the conservative postmaster general, Montgomery Blair to resign.

So, eventually, Fremont left and then Blair resigned. The party finally reunited in time for the 1864 election. It stayed the same in 1864 as it was in 1860, as Lincoln was his strategist for the campaign. He even had a hand in managing the Republican Speakers' Bureau, then advised the state committees on what their campaign tactics should be, fired and hired government employees so he could gain the support of the party, then he did whatever he could to empower all the sailors and soldiers that could to vote. He found that a majority of citizens who wore red uniforms voted Republican. Lincoln won that election by a vast, accessible majority (55%) over Democrat General George McClellan.

The Democrats used for their platform in 1864 a peace conference and an armistice, so, therefore, the prominent Democrats or Republicans demanded Lincoln should heed the Confederate offers of peace, no matter how irregular they appeared.

The Conservatives started protesting to him about the implication that the war should go to free all slaves. In his usual inaugural address, Lincoln promised he would be liberal with the pardons if only the South would stop the war, but he kept insisting on a reunion for a condition if there was any peace arrangement. In his Second Inaugural Address, he expressed the embodiment of his policies by his famous words *"**with malice toward none; and charity for all.**"*

Lincoln's terms did not satisfy the Radical Republicans or the Confederate leaders, so it boiled down to the one fact that there was no peace possible until the Confederacy defeat was final.

As with all things government, either now or then, when the Civil War did end, Lincoln and his policy for the South's defeat was nowhere evident in the details. Lincoln did continue to feel and believe that their primary objective and priority needed to be in restoring the *'seceded states,'* back to their original place in the Union as quickly as possible.

Lincoln had no real fix or uniform program for that region as a whole. States like Tennessee and Louisiana, Lincoln could continue in urging the acceptance of any new governments to set up under the 10% plan he had designed during the Civil War.

For states like North Carolina and Virginia, Lincoln was willing to fall back on the older rebel governments for a temporary means so they could transition from a war setting to a situation of peace. Lincoln was noted as in opposition against 'no strangers' could govern the South.

Lincoln felt that education should be offered to blacks and whites and allowed to go to the same schools. He also thought that the blacks that were extremely intelligent and those who fought in the war should be able to vote.

When it came to reconstruction, Lincoln and those who fell out as extremists in his Republican sector stuck out like a sore thumb in the early part of 1865, worse than they did one year before.

Some Radicals started demanding there should be a time of military supervision over the South, the transferring of political power from the plantation owners to their prior slaves, confiscating the estates and dividing them between the free men.

April 1865 found Lincoln starting to change some of his ideas in regards to some respects, and this helped in narrowing the gap between him and the Radicals. Lincoln went ahead with his permission for assembling the rebel legislature in Virginia; Lincoln approved the principle of Stanton's ideas for the military occupation of the Southern States.

When the Cabinet met April 14th, Attorney General James Speed said that Lincoln seemed to be leaning toward the radical position.

It did not matter because Lincoln kept his eye on what his goal had been all along and that was to restore the United States to a single nation all under the original Constitution. Ending slavery was to be secondary to the first goal. The 13th Amendment that banned slavery through all of the United States passed after Lincoln had pulled enough political strings and granted all the favors needed to get the required *"Aye"* votes — already failing one time in the House, before all of Lincoln's backroom meddling and negotiations. Thaddeus Stevens had to say that the biggest measure of the 19th century would be that this Amendment had been passed by the use of corruption, abetted, and aided by the man considered to be the purest in America.

PART X

———————

STILL MAD ENOUGH TO MURDER

«No man has a good enough memory to be a successful liar.»

Abraham Lincoln

April 14th, 1865, John Wilkes Booth was 26 years old and an advocate for slavery with his ties to the South and the flashy son of the most prominent theatrical families during the 19th century decided he would murder Lincoln.

The assassin that killed Lincoln died April 26th, 1865 was killed near Port Royal, Virginia.

Booth had been number nine out of ten kids born to actor Junius Booth. It was felt he had great potential for the theatre at an early age but was also beginning to show an emotional instability. On top of it all, he was having an issue that made it hard for him in accepting his brother Edwin's claim to fame as a rising actor of that day.

After John had found no success in Baltimore Theaters during 1856, he played some of the minor roles he found in Philadelphia until the year 1859, and he then joined a The Shakespearean stock company there in Richmond, Virginia. John became widely known while on tour in the Deep South during 1860 and the demand remained all through the Civil War. He even had a turn as the lead in "William Shakespeare's *"**Richard III**"* while in New York City during 1862.

Booth being a strong supporter of the Southern cause hated Lincoln. He wanted slavery. By the fall of 1864, Booth started plotting an abduction of none other but Lincoln himself. Booth recruited several men to work with him, and during the winter they worked out several different scenarios. Several attempts they tried, failed, so Booth decided to destroy Lincoln no matter what it would cost.

Booth heard about Lincoln going to the theatre on April 14th, 1865 to see the play '***Our American Cousin***' at Ford's Theatre there in the capital. Booth gathered his band of bad boys and gave everyone their assignments, and they had even planned on murdering the Secretary of State, William Seward. Booth wanted to kill Lincoln himself.

At 6:00 P.M. John Wilkes Booth went into the empty theatre and tampered with the outside door to the presidential box so he could jam it shut once he

got inside. Booth came back during the third act to locate Lincoln and those with him and found them without any guards.

When Booth got inside the theatre box, he pulled out his .44 caliber pistol and shot Lincoln behind his left ear. He fought shortly with Major Henry Rathbone and then jumped over the railing while shouting. He landed/fell hard on the stage which broke a bone in his left leg. There seems to be some argument that some feel the injury did not happen until later.

Booth made his escape through the alleyway with his horse. Trying to kill Seward was a failure, but Lincoln died the next morning.

Booth met up with one of the other in his gang, a David Herold. Booth went on to flee through the state of Maryland. He only stopped to have his leg fixed by a Samuel Mudd, who was supposedly a doctor in Maryland who later would be convicted of conspiracy.

There was a massive manhunt that followed, and a $100,000 reward fueled it. Herold and Booth hid out for days near the Zekiah Swamp in a thicket of trees still in Maryland state.

April 26th the Federal Troops were on the scene at a farm there in Virginia, south of Rappahannock River. Booth was supposed to be hiding out in the tobacco barn there. Herold gave up before they set the barn on fire. Booth still refused to surrender.

Booth was shot, not for sure if, by himself or a soldier, he was carried to the farmhouse porch, where he died. A doctor who had operated on Booth in the past year, ID'd his body, and then it was secretly buried. Four years later they had it reinterred. As always there was no evidence to support that it was John Wilkes Booth that had been killed.

PART XI

ROBERT & HIS DEALINGS WITH MARY TODD

«A man watches his pear tree day after day, impatient for the ripening of the fruit. Let him attempt to force the process, and he may spoil both fruit and tree. But let him patiently wait, and the ripe pear at length falls into his lap.»

Abraham Lincoln

After Lincoln died, Robert resigned from service, and he and his mother, Mary Todd Lincoln moved to Chicago, Illinois where he settled in to practice law.

Robert married a Mary Harlan in 1868, and they had three kids, but their one and only son died when he was a teenager.

His mom's wild spending led him eventually to him having her placed in an insane asylum during 1875. When Robert's aunt, Mary's sister, found out where she was at, she went to the insane asylum and had her released to her care.

Robert was more public-spirited, and he served under President Chester Arthur as the Secretary of War in 1881-85, President James Garfield, and later on, he served as the Minister to Great Britain in 1889-92.

Robert's presence while working during the assassinations of both President William McKinley and Garfield seemed to make him self-conscious about fatalities when attending presidential functions.

For a while, Robert served as the president of the Pullman Company. While there he led a quiet life before dying in 1926, always trying to protect and preserve his father's memory.

Robert was known as a hard-working man, disciplined, confident, strong, self-aware, generous, proper, a real gentleman, kind, witty, and very intelligent. At the same time he could be impatient with others and despised laziness and ignorance, did not like deception and lies when it came to selfish and dishonorable people, and if you ever offended him, he was good at holding a grudge just like his mom's family.

Mary's Charlatans

It seemed Mary Todd started making trouble for President Lincoln as quickly as they moved to Washington. She had, you might say, strong opinions of other people. If she were not able to change Lincoln's mind herself, she would try different routes to get her way.

She was always meddling about how to distribute some of the minor offices and tried to interfere with the assignment of Cabinet members. The people who were around her knew how to flatter her to gain control and influence her.

After Willie Lincoln had died, her situation got even worse in the spring of 1862. Elizabeth Keckley, her seamstress, felt to help Mrs. Lincoln feel better would be for her to see a medium or a spiritualist. These people sure did not improve Mrs. Lincoln's mental stability.

Mary and Abraham Lincoln were communicating with those who had passed on seemed natural to them. President Lincoln even once asked one of the Union officers if he had ever caught himself talking to the dead? He confessed to this young officer that he had found himself involuntarily talking to Willie as if he were next to him ever since Willie had died.

The period President Lincoln was laying in a state before they took him by train to Springfield, Illinois, Mary Lincoln was so frantic in her suffering they had to leave her in her bed.

Mary was obsessed with loving and especially more so with worrying about her children and husband. As it turned out, she had a good reason for the worry. She lost three of four sons, and then her husband being killed. Maybe it was more premonition that caused her fear.

Mary's letters always told about the gossip going on in Washington and Springfield, Ill detailing the news about her children, some of the political activities taking place, and her expressions of pure longing for companionship and intimacy.

There were Nicolay and Hay who had never gotten along with Mary Lincoln. They worked and even slept in the White House, but never ate their meals in the White House.

Because Hay and Nicolay were such close friends to Lincoln, they sometimes would go to the theater if Mary was away from Washington. Hay and Nicolay had been friends forever; before Hay had gone away to Brown University. They both had literary goals, and both admired the President.

Both men were always ready for late night talks to discuss public policy or some political jokes with the President. May 14th, 1864 in Hay's diary he had recorded that the President had come in last evening and told them about his retirement of the enemy at Spottsylvania and the Unions pursuit.

Hay had complimented him on the underpinning he had left, and Lincoln made the comment that he weighed 180 pounds. The stating of that fact is essential due to the situation of his health revealed later in this book.

President Lincoln became extremely depressed over all the death of all the young men who had given their lives for this cause. Lincoln would sit by a window at one end of the White House for hours and hours at a time trying to figure out how to hang himself from the oak tree outside without anyone noticing until it was too late. (Of course, no one at this point knew that Lincoln had had syphilis for quite several years now and one of its symptoms could be depression.) There were some nights that his two closest friends and advisors would take turns sitting with him so he could not harm himself.

Both secretaries got along well with Robert Todd Lincoln when he came home from Harvard on vacation. Mary alienated Nicolay and Hay quickly, and they called her the 'hell-cat' for all her demands. When William Stoddard, the presidential aide prepared to be leaving the White House to go to Arkansas in the fall of 1864, it was John Hay that told Nicolay that he had no idea what they would do after Stoddard was gone. He said that the two of them by themselves could not manage Mary Lincoln. Stoddard was the only one who could ever handle her.

PART XII

LINCOLN'S FINAL HOURS

«When I do good I feel good, when I do bad I feel bad, and that's my religion.»

Abraham Lincoln

The assassination is probably one of the saddest events known to American History.

We find that the morning of April 14th, 1865 was good Friday, and Lincoln got up in a good mood. It had been on Sunday, April 9th that Robert E. Lee had surrendered to Ulysses S. Grant. The famous truce was signed at Appomattox, Virginia at the Court House and signaled an end to the United States most terrible Civil War.

The Lincolns decided to celebrate the end of the war they would go to Ford's Theatre and see *"Our American Cousin."* Lincoln had asked that General Grant and his wife go with them that evening. Grant told him they could not as they were on their way to see their kids in New Jersey.

What appears to make it more ominous is that Secretary of War at the time, Edwin Stanton, begged Lincoln not to go to the theatre as he had a bad feeling of a possible assassination. Mary Todd Lincoln did not want to go either, and she was having another one of her bad headaches. Even Mr. Lincoln fussed about being so tired and exhausted. But, he said, an evening out for comedy would probably help them feel better.

Lincoln had such confidence in his bodyguards and the fact that they would keep him protected that he shrugged off everyone's warnings and even invited Major Henry Rathbone and his fiancée, Miss Clara Harris.

Lincoln's primary bodyguard, Ward Lamon did not go to the play, and John Parker was sent instead. John Parker, a police guard, was known by everyone for his like of whiskey, and he was supposed to be protecting the President? Where was Parker when the President was murdered? He had left his post outside the President's box at the time of intermission to go to the Star Saloon to help with his craving for alcohol.

During the 3rd act, Mary and Abraham were laughing and holding hands when a man ran into the box that was now unguarded. The intruder as you know was the actor, John Wilkes Booth, a Confederate sympathizer. Booth used a Derringer pistol to shoot into the backside of the President's head. Rathbone immediately tried to take down Booth, but Booth was able to overpower him by making a slash to Rathbone's arm with a dagger.

Many have different versions of what he said after Booth shot the President. Some are:

One thing known for sure is that Booth jumped from the President's theatre box onto the stage and as he jumped caught his boot spur on the curtain and caused him to break his left shin. (As you know from above there is some argument to if he broke his left shin at this point or later.) Somehow Booth limped away and made his exit out the stage door, initiating the largest manhunt in American history.

When you think about it, even being in a coma, the real story is the sadness of the hours of pure agony the President had to endure before he expired that early morning April 15th.

Through scientific evidence produced in a prominent medical school in New York today, we find even after being pronounced dead the soul stays in the body for quite some time. Until Lincoln was dead, his soul was still there and could hear all that was being said around him. He had to know he was dying that his vision/dream he had told someone about had indeed come true. While trying to do his very best as the President of the United States, there was still someone who hated him so very much they were willing to take any risk to kill him.

When the audience started crying out that the President had been shot and to catch the murderer, the first doctor to get to the President was Charles A. Leale a 23-year-old Army Captain, he had only graduated with his medical degree six weeks prior.

Dr. Leale was immediately able to assess that the bullet entered the skull behind the left ear and tore into the left side of the brain. Dr. Leale sent out for water and brandy, and by the time he got to President Lincoln, Abraham was already paralyzed, eyes closed, and in a coma. Lincoln's breathing was difficult and noisy but only intermittent. By placing a finger on Lincoln's right radial pulse, there could be no movement of the said artery.

When Leale's fingers had passed over Lincoln's head during the examination, he noticed a *"**large firm clot**"* just one inch under the curved back line at the occipital bone. Dr. Leale removed the clot by wiggling his finger in the hole that the pistol ball had made and realized it had gone into the brain.

Today, this maneuver seems shocking; but at that time doctors had no idea about sterile technique nor microbiology, and it was the standard method used to examine gunshot wounds. It was clear that it was a mortal wound and no going back.

When Lincoln's breathing seemed to be a bit better, and the doctor could get some water and brandy down his throat two more physicians had shown up. The three doctors decided to move the President across the street to a boarding house. He was moved to the upstairs in a Union soldiers room who had stepped out for the evening.

Because Lincoln was so tall, he had to be placed on the bed in a diagonal position. They removed the foot of the bed so he could lie in a more comfortable position. Windows in the room were opened up and everyone except for the doctors, Mary Todd, Robert, their son, and some of Lincoln's devoted advisors, were cleared from the small room.

The doctors tried to get the lead ball out by probing around inside the wound with some surgical instruments and of course unwashed hands. Since surgery of the brain was not a specialty in Lincoln's time, the surgeon's only hope was to keep the wound open so the blood might keep flowing freely so it would not compress Lincoln's brain further and causing more injury. Their efforts, of course, did nothing and as the morning ticked by Lincoln kept declining. It is appalling at the least at what they did not know about medicine at that time. However, from what is described of the damage done inside Lincoln's brain by the bullet, even today there would doubtedly have been any '***bringing back***' with today's medicine.

It was 6:40 a.m., Dr. Leale said that his pulse could not even be counted; it was so intermittent. He could only feel two or three beats that were followed by a long intermission. His breathing got even shorter, and his expirations were longer and so labored while being accompanied by the guttural sounds.

Ten minutes later, Dr. Leale stated that the respirations would cease at times and everyone would look at their watches in the event it might be his last, and then the silence would be broken by an inspiration very prolonged, then followed by a loud expiration.

The President was not in good health, to say the least, and who are we to say that he had that much time left in his remaining presidency. Most people have no idea that during his final living years that there was a high probability that Lincoln did have cancer of his adrenal glands. We also do not know who had the carrier gene for the thyroid cancer which their one son had died. He had syphilis that he thought he had been cured from but certainly was not.

Apparently, it had reached its latent stages by the symptoms Lincoln was exhibiting.

All three doctors examined him, and it was written that President Lincoln had breathed his last at 7:20 a.m. and his spirit fled to God who had given it.

Secretary of War, Stanton saluted his friend and fallen President and uttered that now our President belongs to the ages. Here lies the perfect ruler of men that the world has ever seen.

Three days before he died, Abraham had told his bodyguard Ward Lamon that he had dreamed a funeral had taken place at the White House in the East Room. While he was dreaming, he asked a soldier standing near his casket about who it was that was dead. The soldier informed him it was the President because he had been killed by an assassin.

Mary Todd Lincoln was so beside herself she could not even attend his funeral. To her, life was over. It would be a month before Mary Lincoln could pull herself together enough to get packed and leave the White House. She was in such a state the doctors refused that she be allowed to be moved.

At almost five o'clock May 22, 1865, Mary Lincoln, Tad, Robert, and Lizzie Keckley descended the public stairway and entered a horse-drawn coach.

Let us remember that the real purpose of writing someone's biography is to make the person fully known to those who read all the facts of the hero or heroine that should be told. The whole of their life needs to be told, even the smallest events that include the way they felt, their thoughts, determinations, and deeds. It should be the duty of the writer to make sure everything is told, the good and bad as it makes up the character of the person and what turned them into who they were in life and how their life contributed to the world in which we live. Everyone has a purpose and leaves their imprint on others lives, sometimes, far into the future.

PART XIII

———————

CONCLUSION

If nothing else, the biography of Abraham Lincoln proves that in the United States a man can come from humble, 'very humble' beginnings and through hard work, believing in themselves and perseverance still has the chance to make a difference for themselves, others, their country, and the entire world.

It takes honesty and courage to stand up against the many who may speak out against you as you try to do the right thing. You must keep placing one foot in front of the other and keep living your life honestly, and eventually, others will see that you are a man of honor and look to the future to serve those who have looked up to you.

Lincoln did not live in the lap of luxury even though his wife tried to do so.

Lincoln did not mind living and socializing with the poor and the blacks as he came from such unfortunate beginnings and he understood their different plights.

Did the Civil War and all the effects afterward solve everything? Unfortunately, it seems it did not. Different races seem to be still not able to get along with each other and feel one is more superior or that one race has been through more than the other. Each race has its battle; it feels it is fighting. Sadly enough, we were all created in the same image and race, creed, nor color should not enter into any of it. The Civil War only set the slaves free, but it did not cure the problems of division, it only started them and made them worse.

Lincoln, despite the rumors and the ugly lies, will always be looked upon as one of the greatest presidents in the succession of all presidents of the United States. He will not be looked down nor remembered for some of his peculiarities. Today, it is the way of the world, is it not?

The difference now is we have telephones, Instagram, twitter, facebook, televisions, iphones, ipads and all the other types of communication devices that we know what happens around the world the minute it happens.

The big difference today? Today there is so much backbiting, lying, greed, dishonesty and we seem to be living in a world of entitlement that it makes some of us so very tired. In Lincoln's day, yes there was backbiting, lying, greed, deception, and killing but it was not as easy as it is today to know about everyone else business without all the modern conveniences.

Maybe that was the best time in history to have lived? Let us remember the real purpose of writing someone's biography. The job of the author is to help the reader know better the person we are writing about. To read all the facts that should be told and their imprint on this life. The whole of their life needs to be told, even the smallest points that include the way they felt, their thoughts, their ideas, determinations, good and bad deeds. The writer must make sure it is all told, the good, sad, and the unfortunate as it makes up the character of the person and what turned them into who they were/are in life and how those experiences caused their life to contribute to the world in which we live. Everyone has a purpose in their time on this earth, and each leaves their imprint on others' lives in some way, sometimes that imprint may not be noticed until far into the future. Remember, we have but one chance of traveling through this life to make a difference.

Strengths of Lincoln:

- Calm and enduring and seemed to keep everything held inside. Very patient with all who approached him. Thought before he would answer.
- He was a person who could talk to anyone, any age, any color and understand what they were telling him.
- He had a secure connection with the poor people because he had lived that life and Lincoln knew what it was like to be the poorest of the poor.
- He never felt or acted like he was better than anyone else.
- He built his presidential cabinet with his friends and his enemies.

You can keep your enemies close so you can watch him. • He was keen on strategies for war and for mediating between the parties in Congress to get the votes he needed.

Weaknesses of Lincoln:

- He was not strong as a father figure. He let his children and his wife Mary run over him and get their way.
- It seemed like a young man he was very good at sewing his seed or his oats with the young ladies. It also seemed it was hard for him to turn down an offer by some of the women, Mary Todd for sure requiring them to get married quickly and have a son almost exactly eight months and two weeks to the day they married.
- For the rumors that he also liked gay men, it seemed he did not try very hard to keep this a secret. Everyone around him seemed to know about his '*trists*' while they lived in Washington and they turned their heads.
- He had syphilis which was untreatable at that time, and it made him extremely fatigued, his weight loss, and the depression he suffered.